Can Elephants

MW01206225

STORY BY: ERNIE SNYDER

ILLUSTRATED BY: SUSAN SCHAFER

Copyright © 2020 Ernie Snyder, Susan Schafer

5688 Publishers

Can Elephants Bowl?

ISBN 978-0-578-73488-0

One day an elephant named Bally decided that he wanted to try bowling for the first time.

Bally stomped over to his best friend Bud's bowling alley to get a lane.

Everyone stared as Bally walked in because they had never seen an elephant in a bowling alley.

Bally approached Bud and asked "Can elephants bowl?"
"You would be the first elephant to try, Bally," Bud replied.

The only shoes Bud could find big enough for Bally were.... PIZZA BOXES!

Bally went over and picked out his bowling ball,
it was his favorite color, green.

Bally picked the ball up with his trunk,
swung it way back,
and then threw it as hard as he could down
the lane.
The ball raced down the lane and then....

Crash!!!

"BALLY! YOU BROKE ALL THE PINS!" yelled Bud.
"You cannot bowl with your trunk anymore."

Bally replied, "I am sorry! I will use my ear next time."

Bally picked up his ball again. This time, he wrapped it up in his ear and swung it around and around as fast as he could.

He let it go, and the ball tumbled down the lane followed by a loud....

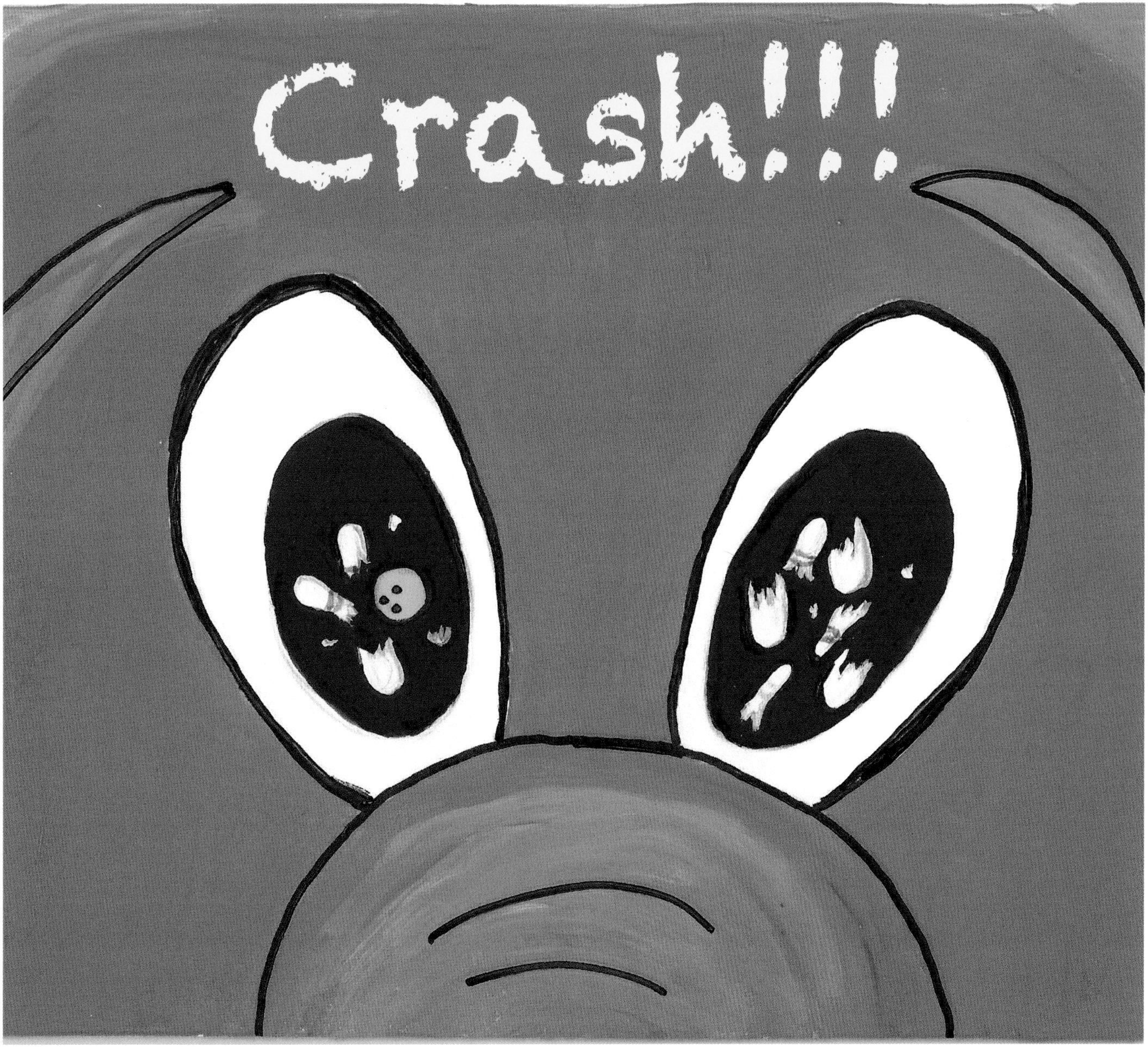
Crash!!!

"BALLY! YOU BROKE ALL THE PINS AGAIN!" Bud hollered.
"Now you cannot bowl with your trunk, and you cannot bowl
with your ears."

"I will try to use my foot the next roll," Bally replied.

Bally pulled the ball back with his foot and gave it a big push down the lane.

Once the ball hit the pins there was yet another loud....

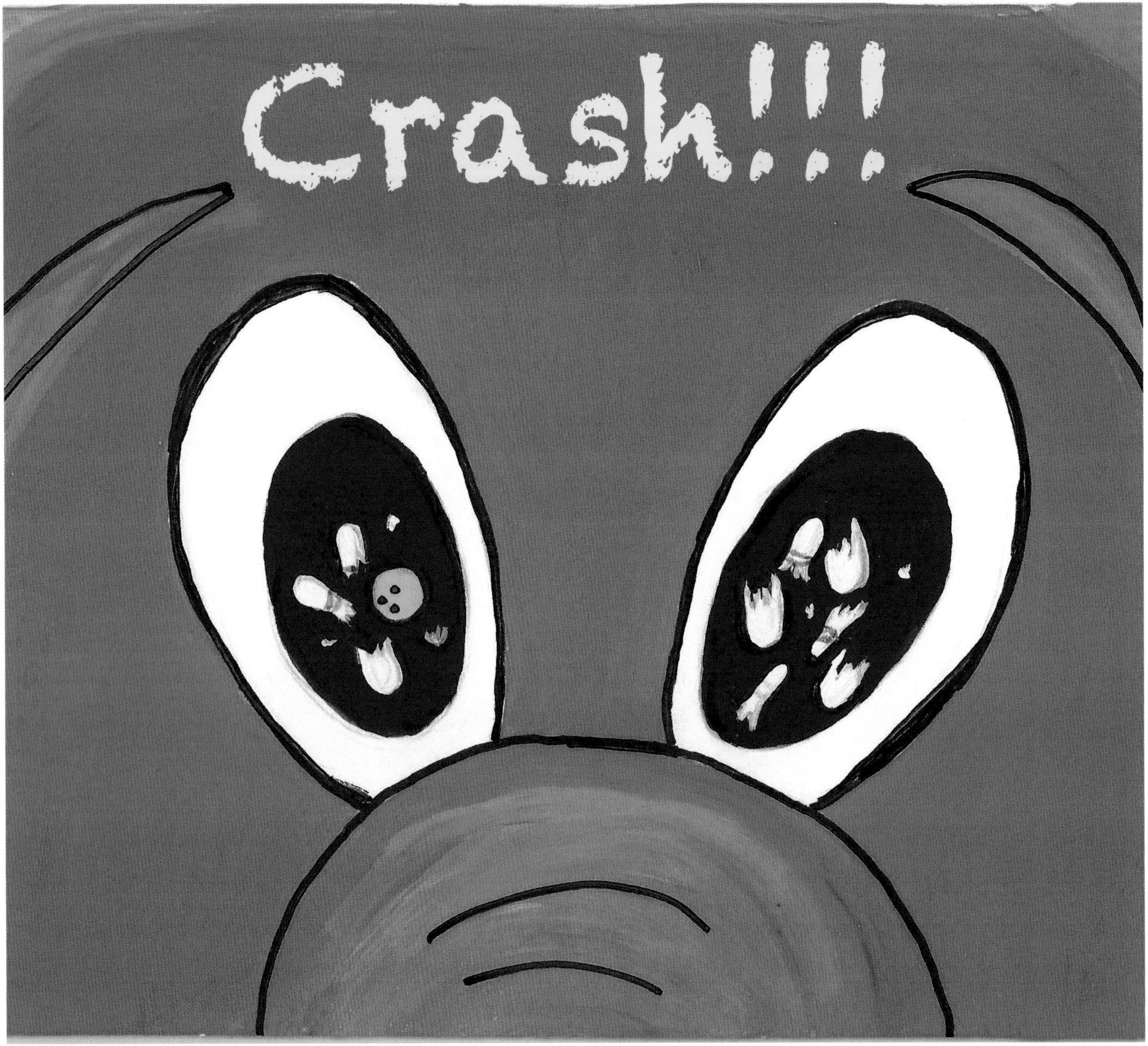
Crash!!!

"BALLY! YOU BROKE ALL THE PINS AGAIN!" shouted Bud.
"Now you cannot bowl with your trunk, you cannot bowl with your ear,
and you cannot bowl with your foot."

Bally answered, "OK, I will try and use my tail."

So Bally set the ball on his tail and began to swing it back and forth as fast as he could. He let the ball go and it zoomed down the lane.

All that could be heard throughout the alley was....

Crash!!!

"BALLY! YOU BROKE ALL THE PINS AGAIN!" Bud exclaimed.
"Wait just a moment, I will be right back."

Bud returned carrying a ramp.
"Here you go Bally, try this. You are too strong for bowling and this
should keep you from breaking any more pins."

Bally picked up the ball, placed it on the ramp, and gave it a gentle push. The ball rolled down the lane just as it was supposed to. There was no crash, and there were no broken pins.

Bally continued using the ramp the rest of the day, laughing and having fun with his new friends.

"I GUESS ELEPHANTS CAN BOWL!" Bud shouted in joy.
"WITH A RAMP!"

About The Author

Ernie Snyder lives in his childhood home in Arvada, CO with his wife, Katy and their four children: Matthew (11), Zachary (10), Sarah (7)and Elizabeth (7). He searcheed high and low for books on bowling to share with the boys when they were 4 and 2 but couldn't find anything. So, one night, putting the boys to bed, he created this story with their help.

About The Illustrator

Susan Schafer is an illustrator, author and art teacher. She credits her blessings and talents to our ultimate creator, God. She is grateful for the family and friends in her life who have encouraged and supported her in her gifts through the years. She enjoys painting, journaling, music and time with friends and family. She is a proud mom to her daughter, Dana. Susan's first book was Impossible the Opossum was released in 2015. She continues to illustrate for others and write stories. Her advice for young and old is to believe that anything is possible!

If you were creating the story, what colors would you choose for Bally?